Things We Do Not Talk About at Dinner

A compilation of poetry written from 2015 to 2022

By

K. Raene

Table Of Contents

Dedicated to Liv, for being someone to show me that there is light in the darkness, that this is not a bad life, just a bad day. For teaching me to spread awareness on depression, check on my friends even on their good days and to be thankful for every day I get with the ones I care about. I miss you dearly, sweet girl.

Dedicated to my mom, husband, and friends for listening to my writings for years and encouraging me even if it brought them to tears.

Dedicated to my little sister for being the brightest sun on my cloudiest days without knowing it.

Dedicated to the counselors and teachers who lead me to graduate high school when I was sure I had no idea what I was doing.

Before you read this, please know there are topics that are not happy on these pages, including self-harm, suicidal thoughts, depression, eating disorders, etc. These are some of my most vulnerable pieces put on paper from the age of 15 to now. Some of them are fiction and popped in my head, others are based on experience. Prepare yourself mentally. Take a break if needed and grab the tissues just in case.

The Feel-Good Stuff

Fallen Angel

With claw marks on her flesh and broken vessels along her spine,

the angel picked her bloodied feathers up and cradled them to her chest.

She knelt to her knees and prayed to herself, for she would be her own savior.

She bathed her wounded wings in the river of the sinners.

She built a home beside the road to hell and served plates to the travelers that passed.

The gates of heaven were not as pearly white as she thought, it was just the reflection of the sun blocking the view of the few who made it in.

The moonlight held her hand during the nights she had screamed at a sky that refused to notice the fear in her eyes.

The yellow roses always bloomed so beautiful during the most painful of months, reminding her to remain standing as tall as they do.

She danced in the fields among those that carried the ugliest of scars. And every evening she listened to those who whispered of what she had done and carved their names into books she had never read.

The Love I Crave

If you hand me a glass half full relationship,

I will pour it down the drain.

Give me an overflowing love and I will drink from it every day.

Soulmates

"My thoughts are troublesome, I cause destruction.

I repeat this to myself at least once a day.

Only because it is the truest thing I have ever known.

My name, my style, my life. One big mess.

Catastrophe upon catastrophe created the world I must live in.

Another fight, another evening painted with red and blue.

Nobody knows what I have seen. Nobody knows what I have been through.

It is why I act so tough. Hence "act", I never want anyone to see me vulnerable.

My sunglasses will hide the tears, the nicotine will stop the shaking.

Mom never seems scared, never seems frightened by anything, never seems fragile.

I learn from her, tucking my sadness into my pocket and hopping into the car with my things.

So, here we are again with the same old story.

But this time is different.

This time I met a boy with past as torn up as mine.

The Girl You Know

I remember she smelled of mint, the gum that was always stuck to her lips, she always blew bubbles when she was deep in thought.

As if a strip of flavor from a gas station could anchor her to reality.

I remember her hair was never quite in the right place.

And although she did not believe in much, you could always find her with her eyes closed at 11:11.

I know that her hands shook violently when she was mad.

As if they were crumbling reminiscence of the earthquake between her teeth. I remember she was stronger mentally than I ever would be physically.

I only saw her break once, but I know she left bruises without touching me.

And she was not confident, but that smile could have shattered the world.

Do Not Fall For A Poet, I Beg Of You.

She will write of every sin you have committed in the language of roses. The world in her eyes will spill onto paper for the world to see.

She will scream her love for you because she only ever speaks adventure. She will tell you your fingertips feel like fire, and she wants to be the sun.

She will not call you handsome or beautiful.

She will trace your lips, plant a kiss, and jot something unusual down on her arm because when she presents herself in anything less than poetry the words fall out like rocks.

She listens to rock. She will seem so soft and unique in a short brown skirt or 90's mom jeans.

She is trying her best to become her own type of aesthetic.

Do not tell her she cannot do anything, or she will do it. Many more times than once.

She plays with animals and starts riots for things she loves.

Because she never understood the term "you fight like a girl."

She fights with a soul that was built from warrior women, messy hair, and endless nights.

Do not fall for a poet because she will be addicted like a drug.

And if you leave her, she will draft a novel about every freckle on your body.

But you will never read it because after the very last sentence is scratched, she will become the sun and place it in a fire or rip it to shreds.

Because a poet is a nightmare and a goddess who walks the street fearlessly.

Sunshine Woman

The sunlight danced in her eyes, water slipping down her back.

The waves were crashing into her as if the ocean were screaming how it had missed her.

It sipped her laughter like fine wine.

The darkness, the sadness, drama and anger was over.

Just the sweet sensation of salty hair and no fears.

The Girl You Know Pt. Two

The universe is a wondrously created place, filled with specks of glitter overhead of marbles circling a huge ball of fire.

Millions of diverse creatures created by the smallest of atoms.

And somehow while adventuring in the chaos, you found her.

The most fractured one of them all.

Broken repeatedly and somehow put herself back together.

But she is so beautifully strange.

Addiction

Good God, you smell like my favorite mistakes.

You look like red and blue lights in the night.

And, you feel like seven shots of vodka, I cannot get enough.

You have all my emotions bundled in the palm of your hand.

My lips ready for another kiss, another sip from the bottle.

You make the worries fade for a while.

Show Me How To Be Brave Like You

A young girl with freckles across the bridge of her nose.

Her eyes are blue, a soft kind like the hijab around her face.

She is calm and quiet.

Her hint of a smile when I told her she could sit by me.

The glisten in her eyes when I told a joke.

When she spoke her language, I was intrigued.

How brave you must be to walk into a high school with only the memories of your country and a pencil.

Star Child

You will never be alone.

The sun will accompany all of your adventures.

The moon has stayed up to listen to your secrets.

The stars give you something to dream for.

You have saltwater and stardust in your body.

Your words are made from the crummy crisp air.

When you die you will only become a different part of this universe.

Honeybee Lady

Her soul is so soft it slips repeatedly though hands.

(Their fault for attempting to hold her entire being)

Honey girl talks smoothly, sweetness sliding down her throat, accent sticking thick to her words.

fluttering around you asks, "Are you okay?" "Are you sure you're okay?" "You don't seem okay."

Her sweaters never cling but simply engulf her smallness in its palm.

And she always wears stripes because it reminds her of how the lines are unstoppable.

They go around and around like her mind.

Her eyes are muddy like the backroads she grew up on.

Sweet like sugar, southern beauty holds her head taller than the tallest sunflowers.

Her ideas are so loud that she must whisper them.

And those legs she balances her tiny torso on are longer than every field she has run through.

But her voice carries so far that every spring and creek ripples when she speaks.

I am my own anthem

My soul is smart, aroused by the smallest hint of an argument.

Sass sits waiting on the back of my tongue.

The ground trembles when I step from my bed in the morning.

Run

I stopped waiting for the storm to pass and became it.

I let the lightning flow into my veins.

Let the thunder scream my name in the sky until people feared the destruction I would leave in my wake.

Phoenix

I crawled through the ashes of my past.

I was reborn in my mistakes.

I forged myself from the fire you started.

I will not apologize for my wings getting in your way.

Fear-less

There is only one person I've known that isn't afraid of anything. Only because he had to face and overcome them all within twenty-two years. And one day he will tell our children what it's like to be truly fearless.

The Not So Happy Stuff

I Found God

when I learned there was not glitter two inches beneath our skin.

She put a hand on my back as I learned

that bruises look like lavender,

but they do not feel as sweet.

She lit the stars a little brighter

on the nights I wanted to join them.

I am starting to feel like the main character of a book someone's writing

Introduction to the life and world of the person

Add a chapter

Plot twist

Another chapter

Kill someone they loved

Another chapter

False love & betrayal

Add a chapter

Include a sprinkle of trauma

Add a chapter

Another plot twist to keep readers interested

Add a chapter

Let them fall in love and then make something bad happen

Add a chapter

When Will You Realize The Difference?

They are taught how to throw knives.

We are taught to keep our keys between two fingers when we go to our car and hope it is sharp enough.

They are taught that we are playing hard to get if we seem uninterested.

We are taught that they are flirting when they are mean to us.

They are taught to shoot guns for fun and hunt any animal that moves.

We are taught to get a gun at 21 because someone could have followed you home.

They are taught that women dress to impress them.

We are taught to cover ourselves up or else someone could take advantage of us.

They are taught to live up their teens and have fun at parties.

We are taught to never give anyone our drink and to always let someone know where you are going.

I Was My Own Bully

Once upon a time I stopped looking in mirrors because I did not like the girl in it.

I hated her so I shut her up. I duct-taped her mouth and refused to let her eat.

I told her that her clothes were too baggy, her face too wide, her skin too jiggly.

I taught her how to play with scissors and kitchen knives and safety pins and pieces of the mirror she broke that one time.

I shoved cruel words down her throat and told her not to believe in God because he did not believe in her.

I gave her trust issues, false hope, and disorders she would have to fight off for years.

I Have Your Drawing Inked Permanently On My Skin Now

I was watching wheel of fortune with my mom and sister when I got the call.

She said you were gone but she was crying, and I was crying, and the tears ended the call for me.

and suddenly all the air that was sitting comfortably in my lungs exploded in my chest and killed my heart with the attack.

I grasped at the floor to try to grab you or your memory.

I tried to scream at God to bring you back. I did not understand how it could happen.

One day we are graduating.

The next I am still trying to believe you will not be at the high school reunion.

I remember the brown bag, the air on my neck, the cold rag, the constant screams and tears, the air refusing to come back to me.

I remember my little sister telling me it is okay and rubbing my back as I left mascara on her shirt and all I could think was who would comfort your siblings.

It must have been so hard to leave everything behind.

I am so sorry you thought that was the only way out.

The Definition Of A Father: Someone Who Stays

How do you forget your own blood?

How do you erase the very creature you wrote on paper?

Your skin tone is hidden deep within me, and I still remember your voice.

How do you stop calling a child you helped create?

Tell me, what is a good age to pretend I never existed?

21 years and you have the nerve to call yourself my father?

You are merely another cell in my body compared to the work my mother had to do.

You do not get to choose which daughters to keep or give away like old clothes rotting in the closet.

You do not get to believe that child support is anything more than a stranger giving me money.

You were not the one to cheer me on at my graduation nor walk me down the aisle at my wedding so how can you carry yourself with the definition of a father.

Crying Is A Weakness

You say I am mean.

You say I am heartless, but I had one yesterday.

You say I do not have a reason to be so rude.

You say that I have too much of a soft soul to try and be so tough.

So, I suppose you never really knew me.

Because if you did,

You would know that I put up a wall when I feel small.

That by having no filter, I can be reckless.

That if a soft girl yells, you never really hear her.

Because if you cannot control me then you will listen to what I have to say.

That everyone who knows me understands I will always choose

having bloody knuckles over a tear

slipping down my cheek.

Panic Attack

My thoughts are blue and purple and the many colors of a bruise.

A broken vessel under the skin.

Because I am not being a useful vessel to my mind.

My chewed-up words spit out like broken teeth.

Small crescent moons line the palms of my sweaty hands from gripping and ungrasping.

And I am sure I have lost calories from the many miles I have run shaking my knees in this blue plastic chair.

But I am dragging my way to the finish line so maybe I can hear you over the thump thump pounding in my ear because my heart has a fear of falling and climbed the jungle gym of my ribs to cling onto the back of my eyes.

And that is why my visions so blurry.

That is why I cannot seem to find the right thing to say.

Not that I did not prepare for this, but my preparations are pinned under this cold metal leg that keeps poking the calf of mine.

But I cannot pry it out because I am busy biting a new hole into my lip.

And so, I pick my teeth up off the floor and place them back and smile like you have just sat a cake down and yelled "MAKE A WISH!!"

But my only wish is to taste air and not the blood on the back of my tongue.

Arachnid Pulse

Do not ask me to say I love you back or expect me to strum the strings of your heart the right way

or that a beautiful symphony will flow out of my mouth.

Because that is not me.

It is a voice with no feeling.

It is a beautiful mess of lies that you happened to land in.

And I am the poisonous spider with which you are stuck.

Short Story (fiction)

You said you would not leave. You said you would love me forever and ever. You promised me.

One day we would be in a house by the ocean where the breeze could blow through our windows.

Where our love would be tasted as much as the salt in the air.

Up all night on the roof asking questions and planning our life together.

And on the bad days we would still hold each other because we knew everything would be okay. We just have to get to the house by the ocean.

But you slammed the doors shut. You tore the house down. You took everything away from me.

If I would not have gotten mad, you would not have driven in the night to calm down. That tree would not have grabbed your car.

So now my plans were replaced with a cross on the highway.

Now, if I ever hear waves crashing, I am afraid I will think of your laughter. And if I walk through the sand on some forgotten beach then I am sure I will think of your smile on my skin.

It will burn more than the sun ever could.

Because we will not have early morning kisses, sipping coffee watching the sunrise.

Because, you are gone, and the sea is inside of me now, it just keeps slipping out with the sobs.

I have begged every star in the sky to bring you back to me.

You did not keep your promise and you did not get to see our house by the ocean.

A Janky Poem I Wrote In Eighth Grade Science Class

Love is hard to capture, a bird that is always free.
But once you mess with trust you cut off its wings.
It cannot fly away, and you locked the door,
how will the bird know its worth anymore?
That it is special, unique, unlike the rest,
because without trust there is nothing left.
You cannot mess up or the bird will run away,
with no love there is not a reason to stay.

The Girl In My Head

She has black hair and green eyes that pierce.

She has scars on her chest and her hands, feet, and eyes.

Her mouth is sown shut, bleeding.

Her teeth are chipped, her tongue has bite marks, and her skin is frail and picked at.

She screams all day for hours.

Throws every shelf down, bloodies her knuckles, wears clothes that cover it all.

You see, the pretty little demon in my head has never known love.

She knows "pig" "anorexic" and more.

She sobs in the corner of my heart and sinks into my feet for the day.

I can tell you what it is like to cry from nightmares.

I cannot tell you what it is like to wake up with a will to live.

In The Dustpan

I used to slice my arms and thighs with pieces of my broken heart.

I have seen a kaleidoscope of love, passion, hurt and fear.

I know that I have tasted sadness without opening my mouth.

That I have held a broken body crying their soul onto my shirt.

My mother was always good at sweeping up people's thoughts and putting them back together. I suppose mine are still in the dustpan.

Life Raft

A storm had begun to form.
When the waves started crashing,
is when I had fallen overboard.
My lungs remained silent,
they knew they had no room.
My thoughts were covered in water,
choices made would not matter soon.
The boat was getting distant,
aboard were the ones who claimed to care.
I reached out for you as a life raft,
hoping for a taste of air.
But I was so consumed in escape,
did not realize the mess I had made.
These arms of mine had splashed so much,
I could not hear the yell.
My mind was so focused on you,
I did not notice who else needed help.

It Will Not Hurt Forever

Your heart is going to shatter.

It will completely obliterate before you are seventeen.

You will sit on your bedroom floor accompanied only by memories.

You will sob and eat sweets and sop around the house in a blanket.

You will get mad and yell and hit your pillow.

You will debate whether you should text them or not.

Your best friend will pep talk you on the phone.

And eventually you will get over it.

Because it feels like Hell. Because it feels like I am trapped in skin that does not fit me. Because I cannot go home. Because I do not have a home.

So, here I am suffocating with thoughts of things going wrong.

Because it is a game. How long can you go without eating? How deep can you cut?

Because he left me. Because he chose a different family.

Because I am mourning the loss of someone who is still alive.

Because nobody is there to hold me. Because I am always panicking.

Because I am the strong one. Filled with "you're going to go far" and "don't let them get to you".

Because their whispers and laughter taste like gasoline. Because I suffer day after day and those candy-colored pills are not working.

Because one time I prayed not to wake up. Because the only ones who love me are miles away.

Because of the semi-colon on my wrist. Because the words will not come out.

Because if they, do I sound like a fragile little girl. Because the world grabbed me by its claws and told me I am not good enough.

Because I do not like this feeling. Because every time I open my eyes, I am scared.

Because I do not believe in being afraid. Because I cannot admit it. I cannot tell others.

Because my scars grow from the inside out. Because I am in constant battle with myself.

Because I am broken. Because I am hidden.

Because I was so quiet today, when I said "Thank You" to the boy, I jumped.

Because I am only a teenager. Because instead of driving a car I am wishing to be hit by one.

Because I said I would stop, and I did not. Because I am the goddess of breaking things.

Because my newly bought jacket was stolen. Because when I go outside, I breathe in ice cubes and police sirens.

While you are up rambling, I am losing feeling in my fingertips from spilling ink on a dead tree.

Because I, the uncontrollable, lost control of myself.

Because I try to write my thoughts on something other than my skin.

Because I dug the razor too deep too many times to still be here.

God gave everyone a mission; I suppose mine is to stay alive.

The Terrified Hurricane

When you speak to me, I start hearing the thunder crack behind my eyes.

I swear I taste lightning on the edge of my tongue.

I want to speak; I want to scream with all the wind force in my soul.

But I know that every time that I do, I will only drown in my own storm.

Fake Smiles

You do not really know me though you think you do.

Have you climbed into my mind; felt the pain I have been through?

You do not know me until you've sunken into my ears, too many cruel words, I fear.

You do not know until you have seen the feelings stuck inside my throat.

Until you have touched my face that tears already coat.

You do not know until you dive into the depths of my smile,

find out I have been waiting for a change a while.

You do not know until my voice cracks when I try not to cry,

that my wish at 11:11pm was to die.

You do not know until you hold me while I shake,

or tell me it will be okay after I break.

You do not know that in myself I am the only one believing.

That "I love you" just means they are leaving.

Messy

I crumple receipts, order tickets, pens and money in my pocket instead of organizing. My clothes lay on the floor of my room, my cash is strewn across the house, my belongings tossed in random places. In a way, I feel that is how my brain is. I shove all my feelings in a pile and swear to sort it all out later, knowing I'll just push it to the side.

Childhood

I wonder what we would've done differently if we knew our last day playing in the neighborhood would be the last. Do you think we would've climbed the highest tree? Stayed out later than the streetlights? Ran around the block as fast as we could, knowing we both had asthma? Jumped in the ditch after it rained one more time? Would we have lit another fire? Talked about what we would do after graduating? Plan a sleepover full of late night pancakes and horror movies we could never finish with the lights off?

As you placed your head in the crook of my neck, I learned that excuses weren't working. As you bit into my collarbone with alligator teeth, I memorized how sharp they were on unwanting skin. As my head hit the window and my lungs collapsed, you taught me to never trust again. As the doors locked and the radio grew louder, you taught me what it was like to be terrified. As I realized a year later that I was not alone in being your "almost" victim, I woke after nightmares of your face. As the officer said "this won't really hold up in court without evidence or a witness, I'm gonna be honest with you." I wished someone had saw you be a monster.

- To the person who opened their truck door at just the right time. I'll forever be grateful to you for saving me and you'll never know.

Anger

I apologize for wearing the hatred I carry for you so boldly on my sleeve rather than tucking it in my pocket like you do. I do not apologize for the names I have called you, the prayers I have wasted on you to disappear, and the strength it took me to rebuild the hope of a woman you broke in front of me.

To The Group Home Kids

For thirty six days, I lied that my name was Rae. I made up stories about where I came from and where I was going. I didn't speak for nearly half of those days. I apologize for not sharing my whole story. Please know I never forgot any of you. I know who I gave my stuff to before leaving. I know who shared the room next to me. I know who watched a scary movie with me when we were allowed. I forgive the girl who bullied me, I know it was because that's all you've known from home. I know who told people she was my other little sister and I protected her like she was. I remember the talks we had about your upbringing. I remember the twelve year old who had spent three years of her life in a house of nine other girls. I remember the substitutes who let us have a little extra phone time, a little extra outside time, and let us watch television. I remember the coach who let me read a book instead of playing dodgeball with kids who didn't like me. I remember the teacher who told me stories about her life in Africa. I think of you all here and there and wish the best for the people I'll never see again.

My brain categorized food with

<u>Reward</u>

Instead of

<u>Necessity</u>

So now I am trying to write a list of reasons I deserve to eat dinner tonight because my sticks and stones body brings me more serotonin than a good meal could.

Why does my mind set up time-outs on nutrition as a punishment?

I swear that I am trying but I think I'm programmed differently than you are because I spend my time arguing with my own organs.

My mind uses their compliments as bullets in a gun that I don't control. I use the scale as a trigger.

The Controversial Stuff

A Letter From Generation Z

(Aka the ones born directly before or up to 11 years after a terroristic bombing.)

You cannot plant a flower and then get mad at it for learning to grow. You cannot throw a seed into a forest fire and get frustrated when it shares its water with other flowers. You cannot chop a branch off a tree and get upset when it learns to adapt and improve its ability to live. You tossed us into an ocean that was drowning in oil that you spilled and yell at us for continuing to clean it up. This world we never asked to live in is begging not to be sent to its grave while you are inventing better shovels to dig with. We are running to the stand of the dead man walking only to realize the executioner is our parents and grandparents. Do you want to know why we are considered the loneliest and most depressed generation now? We were born into a historical moment of fear and death. While you watched the planes hit on national television, our brains were memorizing your screams and the way you shook while you held us. Until all we knew about that day was terror and the fear of the unknown. Some of you embedded your hate into your precious flowers, so that every hijab they saw was the pilot of that plane. While you watched the war the next two years, wondering when we would get hit, you seemed to have forgotten the sponge that sat on the couch beside you, while you spat those hateful disgraceful words about how Muslims wanted to kill us all. In that moment, you were attempting to burn the love for others we had hidden in our soil. We saw when women had to fight back against the government, threatening to take away the rights of their bodies in 2004. We were there, though most in elementary school when Hurricane Katrina slammed into the gulf, demanding to devour the residents of those homes. While we ate dinner, we watched the news showing us dead bodies, animals that did not know how to swim and people crying for their loved ones. This is when we learned that our planet would fight back with every swing, we threw at it. Our ears were present when the first African American president was elected, and the hate that was jabbed at him had nothing to do with his political party and more to do with white people needing an excuse to use the N word. We heard the things adults were saying when they were not in church. We saw when a fun run turned into a run for their lives in Boston. That was the day we realized not every seed grows from love. When people marched in defense of the only planet we have, begging for people to care so that future generations could live, we saw the continued purchases of plastic as if to say, 'we heard you, we just don't care.' Your LGBT+ kids that were struggling to breathe in a world of 2 genders listened to every sentence you spoke when they finally allowed two people that loved each other to get married. That was the day we learned what a closet was and why it was easier to hide then open the door to face you. We stood when women had to fight back against the government, threatening to take away the rights of their bodies in 2017. That was the day that instructed little girls they are a mere flower compared to a forest of men. We stood again when women had to fight back against the government, threatening to take away the rights of their bodies in 2018. When a disease flipped the entire world upside down, we struggled to continue with our education on a computer screen in the same four walls, for multiple months, not allowed to go outside, not allowed to see our friends, forced to understand what we could from our teachers online rather than in a classroom. While you figured out how to progress as an already accomplished adult, our young brains were crying out for normalcy. While our friends' grandparents, siblings, and parents were saying goodbye to them over video chat, we heard you say how it was never real. When we stood beside our Black friends as they chanted for change, as they yelled for the brutality to stop, we watched as you pretended you did not see it. As the deaths increased, as the protests increased, we memorized what you looked like as a word that should not be a part of your vocabulary fell out of your mouth repeatedly. We are still picking up the pieces of friendship, peace, and trust to a puzzle our ancestors tore apart, so not your grandparents do not get a free pass because they were there during segregation and racism. They have had over sixty years to adapt and change. It is their fault for burning the branch that was chopped off. And now, we watch again as a country goes to war and wait for us to be next in the firing lane.

Take this as a warning from the mouths of your babes, past generations. We will not stand aside and watch the ground crumble from beneath our feet. We are the most educated generation yet. We will use those diplomas to set fire to the hate laced words in your brains. We are the most diverse generation. We will stand next to our Hispanic friends, Black friends, Mixed friends, Immigrant friends, anything but white friends as they push back against your bigoted racism. Most of you mumble made up messages about technology ruining our lives, yet you are the ones who created it in the first place. Please think before you speak about things you set up for our failure. You say you do not want gun control, because it offends your rights but when we cannot remember math problems, we remember to stay down low, turn off the lights and keep a textbook in your backpack so the bullet will not go too far. We have lived through news stories of 107 mass shootings, 230 schools since columbine and you wonder why we are curious of why you would need an AK47. You say it is your rights until you are getting a message from your child "If I don't make it, I love you and I appreciated everything you did for me." A student in Florida in 2018, 17 people dead, fourteen injured. "Mom there is a shooting. Mom help," a student in Texas in 2021. Four injured. "Mom I am okay there was a shooting right outside my classroom. I am not sure what happened yet. I cannot call you yet, but I am really scared." A student in New Mexico in 2017. Two dead. Please remember to tell those parents your thoughts on the matter. We are the children of the ones that tried to make things better but needed a little help. We were born to make this place a better home for our children. We will be the flowers that created gardens instead of forest fires that destroyed innocent lives. We were raised during protests, politics, and war. When will you understand that we are not going backwards? We stand tall, hold our voices louder and carry our kindness as a weapon. If you want to continue your legacy of hatred, I will consider adapting to the world we are creating from your destruction before you get lost in the ashes.

Pro-None Of Your Business

Feel the anger of the women who stood before you seep into the soil.

Where the nurses who mended your war wounds lay.

Where the ones who birthed your leaders lay.

Where the ones who held those signs fifty years ago lay.

What good it did them if we are still not being allowed to have rights of our own bodies.

The term you are looking for is “livestock.”

So, herd us into the pen, lay your weapons against our temples and remind us that our organs are already spoken for by a god only half of us believe in.

When you crucify us for having to make a choice you had no part in, will you nail us to the same cross you did him?

Funny how he heard your cries but did not hear mine.

My uterus got in the way.

When you sign that law into place, hope you remembered the woman who taught you to write.

When you drag her to your police car for speaking up, hope you know who crafted those hands you grabbed her with.

When you scream into their faces, hope you picture the woman who created thc lungs you are using.

Fussy Sins

To the boy who treats sexualities like a religion he does not want to follow.

To the girl following a loving God telling girls holding hands how they will burn in hell.

To my friend that would never look me in the eyes if I told her I signed a transgender rights petition.

To the people I lost when I said marriage is not just a man and woman.

To the preacher's wife who looked nauseous when I said love is love.

To the man who could not believe a "Christian like me" supported it.

You will not phase me. You will not stop me. You will not even slow me down.

Because I was raised in a town with the bible belt wrapped so tight around it, we could not breathe without choking on another bible verse.

Without a single gay person in my entire family, they attempted to plant seeds of judgement in my brain.

I heard more homophobic slurs in my family than I did at a public school.

As if to say God wanted us to love everyone except them.

In eighth grade, I earned a pansexual friend, transgender friend and met a lesbian for the first time.

I burned the whole forest down.

Because although we do not agree on the same things, my family also taught me I was born with a voice for a reason.

Black Lives Matter

How has it been nearly 200 years and you still pick and choose based on skin color? You say our fight is stupid, but you don't get what we are fighting for. I have white privilege. It doesn't mean I want it but it means I must use it to do what is right. "But I don't make a lot of money?" It has nothing to do with money, and more to do with being able to walk outside and do normal daily routines without fearing for our lives.

Can you hold a bag of skittles while walking down the street?

Trayvon Martin, shot dead, age 17.

Can you hold a cell phone in your own garage?

Andre Hill, shot and handcuffed, death by bleeding out, age 47.

Can you walk home from a grocery store?

Manuel Ellis, beaten to death by cops, age 33.

Can you sleep in your home?

Breonna Taylor, shot 8 times and killed, age 26.

Can you sit in your own home?

Atatiana Jefferson, shot and killed through her window, age 28.

Can you stand in your grandmas backyard?

Stephon Clark, shot at more than 20 times and killed, age 22.

Can you eat ice cream on your couch at your house?

Botham Jean, shot and killed, age 26.

Can you make a mental health call to 911?

Michelle Cusseaux, shot and killed, age 50.

Tanisha Fonville, shot and killed, age 20.

Can you walk down the stairs in your apartment building?

Akai Gurley, shot and killed, age 32.

These are a few reasons that we stand tall.

Therefore I will not be quiet.

This is why I will put my body between an innocent person of color and a uniform.

Because blue and black haven't proven to mix well together.

You want our generation to trust the ones that kill our friends, teachers, neighbors, etc.?

We see more "accidental murders" on the news than actual charges placed on the badges.

Does the melanin in their skin tone scare you? If they get a good job does it make them more approachable? Does their language make you uncomfortable when you aren't using it to sound cool in front of your friends? Accept that you weren't raised being taught how quickly your life can be taken if you make one wrong move, and use your comfortability to press the issue into the white guys who run our country.

The End

I would like to personally thank you for reading my barest thoughts on paper. I have been writing poetry since I was fourteen, I am glad people will now read it. Most of these are from just randomly getting the urge to write. I hope they mean something to someone who reads them. I hope to one day be a well-known poetry and fiction novel author. Remember yourself as one of the first to purchase my first book. You are going down in history as we speak. Live every day like it's your last.

Cheers

to new beginnings,

K. Raene

www.ingramcontent.com/pod-product-compliance
Lightning Source LLC
LaVergne TN
LVHW050343160826
845677LV00014B/3760

* 9 7 9 8 8 4 1 6 4 7 1 0 2 *